Materials

Rubber

by Mary Firestone

Consultant:
Kevin D. Ott
Vice President, General Products Group
Rubber Manufacturers Association
Washington, D.C.

Capstone
press
Mankato, Minnesota

First Facts is published by Capstone Press
151 Good Counsel Drive, P.O. Box 669, Mankato, Minnesota 56002
www.capstonepress.com

Library of Congress Cataloging-in-Publication Data
Firestone, Mary.
    Rubber / by Mary Firestone.
      p. cm. —(First Facts. Materials)
    Includes bibliographical references and index.
    Contents: Rubber—What is rubber?—Natural rubber—Synthetic rubber—Qualities of rubber—Rubber's many uses—Rubber surfaces—Recycling rubber—Amazing but true!—Hands on: dandelion latex.
    ISBN 0-7368-2652-1 (hardcover)
    1. Rubber. I. Title. II. Series.
TS1890.F54 2005
678'.2—dc22   2003027838

Summary: Discusses features of rubber including how it is manufactured and made into useful products we use every day.

Editorial Credits
Christopher Harbo, editor; Jennifer Bergstrom, series designer; Molly Nei, book designer; Scott Thoms, photo researcher; Eric Kudalis, product planning editor

Photo Credits
Capstone Press/Gary Sundermeyer, front cover, 5, 6–7, 14, 15, 16–17
Cheryl R. Richter, 19
Corbis/Brownie Harris, 13; Claudia Kunin, 20; Eye Ubiquitous: David Cumming, 9; Royalty-Free, 11
Index Stock Imagery/Inga Spence, 8
Photodisc, back cover, 1
Visuals Unlimited/Inga Spence, 18

Capstone Press thanks the Lake Crystal Area Recreation Center for its help with a photo shoot for this book.

1 2 3 4 5 6 09 08 07 06 05 04

Table of Contents

Rubber

Sara is almost done making her picture. A rubber band holds her colored pencils together. Her rubber stamps lie nearby. Sara uses an eraser to remove one last line from the picture. Rubber is in many things people use every day.

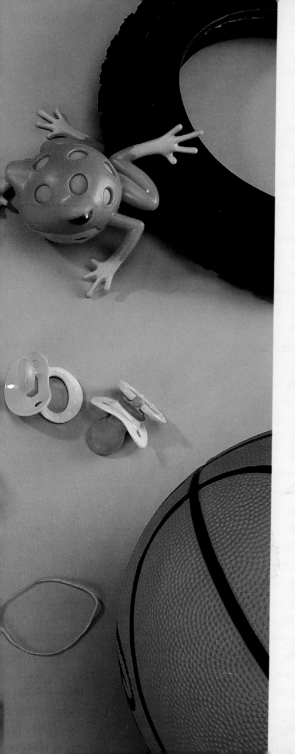

What Is Rubber?

Rubber can be **natural** or **synthetic**. Natural rubber comes from hevea trees. These trees grow in rain forests. People make synthetic rubber with chemicals. People use many things made with both types of rubber.

Natural Rubber

Workers gather **latex** from hevea trees. They cut a small line in the bark. Latex drips out. Workers collect the latex, dry it, and send it to rubber factories.

Workers mix natural latex with **acid** to make rubber. The acid turns the tiny rubber pieces into clumps. Rollers press the clumps into sheets.

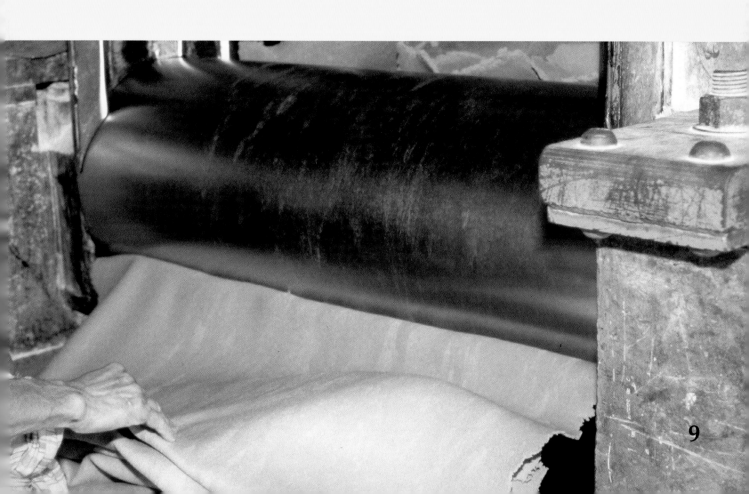

Synthetic Rubber

Factories make synthetic rubber. Chemicals are mixed together to make liquid latex. The latex is mixed with acid to make rubber crumbs. The crumbs are washed, dried, and pressed into **bales**. Factories use the rubber to make shoe soles and other products.

Qualities of Rubber

Rubber has useful **qualities**. It can hold air. Bicycle tires and inner tubes are made of rubber. Electricity cannot pass through rubber. Electricians wear thick rubber boots and gloves. Rubber keeps people safe from electric shocks.

Fun Fact!
Tires are made by mixing natural and synthetic rubber.

Rubber's Many Uses

Rubber is used in many products. Boots and the bottoms of shoes are often made of rubber. Rubber keeps feet dry.

Rubber is also used to make bicycle brakes. Rubber brake pads rub against the wheel. They slow down the bicycle.

Rubber Surfaces

Rubber is used under artificial turf in football and baseball fields. The rubber makes the ground feel softer when players fall. Some running tracks are made of rubber. Rubber tracks are softer under runners' feet.

Fun Fact!
Stephen Perry from England received a patent for a rubber band in 1845.

17

Recycling Rubber

Rubber can be **recycled**. Recycling centers break up old tires. The pieces are cut up and made into new things.

Some play areas
use recycled rubber
on the ground for
safer falls. Recycled
rubber is also used
for home roofing.

Fun Fact!
Recycled rubber
is used to make
floor mats in cars.

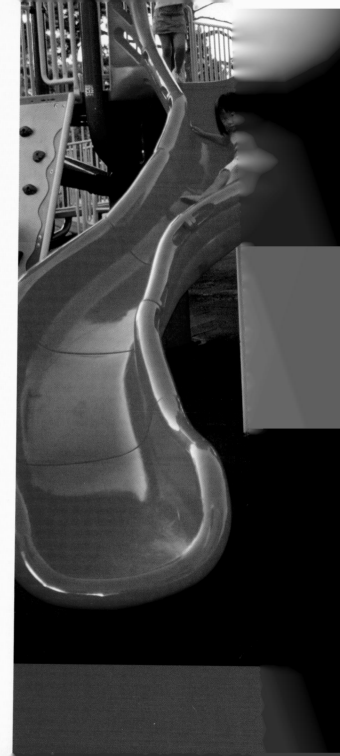

Amazing but True!

Bubble gum is made with rubber. Rubber makes gum chewy. It keeps the gum from breaking apart as it is chewed. Rubber also lets the gum stretch without breaking. The gum stretches when it is blown into big bubbles.

Hands On: Dandelion Latex

Latex can be found in dandelions. You can make your own latex ball with dandelion stems.

What You Need

20 dandelions
plate
paper
pencil

What You Do

1. Collect 20 dandelions.
2. Break the flowers off the stems.
3. Firmly slide your fingers down each dandelion stem. Squeeze the white liquid from the stems onto a plate. The white liquid is latex.
4. Wait a few minutes to let the latex dry. It will change from white to clear.
5. Scrape the latex off the plate with your fingers. Roll it between your fingers to make a ball.
6. Try bouncing your latex ball. Does it bounce?
7. Draw a line on a piece of paper with a pencil. Try erasing the line with the latex ball.

Glossary

acid (ASS-id)—a liquid chemical that is mixed with latex to make rubber

bale (BALE)—a large bundle; synthetic rubber is pressed into bales.

latex (LAY-teks)—a milky liquid that comes from certain plants or is made from chemicals

natural (NACH-ur-uhl)—found in or produced by nature rather than being made by people

quality (KWAHL-uh-tee)—a special feature of something or someone

recycle (ree-SYE-kuhl)—to make used items into new products; people can recycle items such as rubber, glass, plastic, and aluminum.

synthetic (sin-THET-ik)—something that is made by people rather than found in nature

Read More

Llewellyn, Claire. *Rubber.* Material World. New York: Franklin Watts, 2002.

Oxlade, Chris. *Rubber.* Using Materials. Chicago: Raintree, 2004.

Internet Sites

FactHound offers a safe, fun way to find Internet sites related to this book. All of the sites on FactHound have been researched by our staff.

Here's how:
1. Visit *www.facthound.com*
2. Type in this special code **0736826521** for age-appropriate sites. Or enter a search word related to this book for a more general search.
3. Click on the **Fetch It** button.

FactHound will fetch the best sites for you!

Index